INSIDE!

100% FOOTBALL ACTION EVERY WEEK!

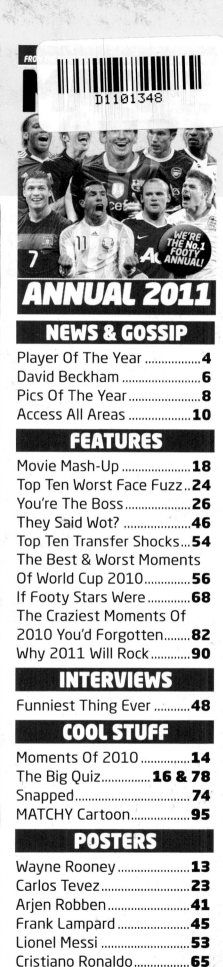

WE'RE THE No.1 FOOTY ANNUAL!

ANNUAL 2011

YOU'RE THE BOSS 26

SNEIJDER 4

WORLD CUP 56

2010'S CRAZY MOMENTS 82

MOVIE MASH-UP 18

Disney · PIXAR
ROY STORY

TOP TEN 24

SNAPPED 74

MATCH! MATES WITH THE STARS! OUT EVERY TUESDAY!

WESLEY SNEIJDER...
PLAYER OF THE YEAR!

The Inter Milan and Holland midfielder was on fire in 2010!

Lionel Messi grabbed the goals in La Liga, while Wayne Rooney and Didier Drogba bossed the Premier League, but Wesley Sneijder had an unforgettable year. MATCH tells you why the Inter Milan midfield hero should be crowned the best player on the planet in 2010!

MEGA GAMBLE!

After two years in Spain, Sneijder left Real Madrid to join Jose Mourinho's Inter Milan. Just hours after signing for the Serie A giants, Sneijder was in the line-up that beat city rivals AC!

TREBLE TIME!

'The Sniper' popped up with decisive goals as Inter stormed to a league, cup and Champions League treble. He ended the season with four goals and six assists from 24 Serie A games!

EURO KINGS!

Sneijder was even more impressive in the Champions League. He hit big goals against Dynamo Kiev, CSKA Moscow and Barcelona as Inter lifted the trophy for the first time since 1965!

WORLD STAR!

Sneijder scored five goals at World Cup 2010, including two in the quarter-final win over Brazil, as Holland reached the final. They lost 1-0 to Spain, but Wes was named in the FIFA All-Star Team!

CLASSIC QUOTE!

Wes on his second goal against Brazil, *"It was my first headed goal and I don't think it will happen again. It just slipped off my bald head and went into the net!"*

DAVID BECKHAM...
ENGLAND LE

MATCH looks back on David Beckham's Three Lions career!

Three Lions boss Fabio Capello has announced that Beckham's international career is over, so MATCH picks out the biggest moments from the legendary midfielder's 14 amazing years in an England shirt!

FUTURE STAR

Becks burst on to the scene after Euro '96 when Glenn Hoddle called him up for a 3-0 win over Moldova in a World Cup qualifier!

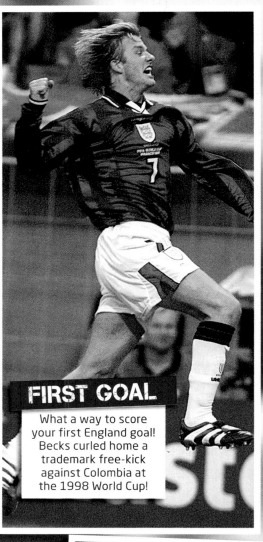

FIRST GOAL

What a way to score your first England goal! Becks curled home a trademark free-kick against Colombia at the 1998 World Cup!

THE RED MIST

No-one will ever forget Becks getting sent off as England crashed out of the 1998 World Cup against Argentina!

LAST-GASP HERO

Beckham's stoppage-time free-kick against Greece in 2001 is one of the best England goals ever, and it put the Three Lions on the plane to World Cup 2002!

GEND!

ENGLAND

ARGIE REVENGE

Four years after his red card in France, Becks slammed home the winning penalty against big rivals Argentina at the 2002 World Cup!

END OF AN ERA

After England were knocked out by Portugal at the 2006 World Cup in Germany, a tearful Beckham stood down as Three Lions captain!

CENTURY BOY

Becks won his 100th cap against France in 2008, then played his last game for England in a 3-0 win over Belarus in 2009!

BECKHAM FACTPACK

Position: *Midfielder*
Club: *LA Galaxy* **Age:** *35*
Caps: *115* **Won:** *68*
Lost: *21* **Goals:** *17*
Yellow cards: *16*
Red cards: *2*

PICS
OF THE YEAR!

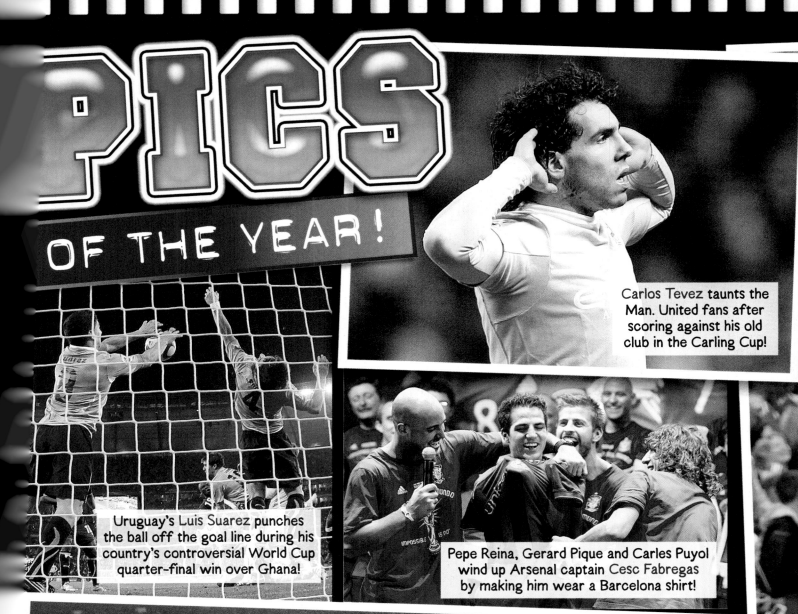

Carlos Tevez taunts the Man. United fans after scoring against his old club in the Carling Cup!

Uruguay's Luis Suarez punches the ball off the goal line during his country's controversial World Cup quarter-final win over Ghana!

Pepe Reina, Gerard Pique and Carles Puyol wind up Arsenal captain Cesc Fabregas by making him wear a Barcelona shirt!

Lionel Messi celebrates the second of his four goals against Arsenal in the second leg of last season's Champions League quarter-final!

John Terry leads the celebrations as Chelsea take an open-top bus tour around London after clinching the Premier League and FA Cup double!

DOUBLE WINNERS

09 CHELSEA FOOTBALL CLUB **10**

Frank Lampard is denied a goal as England crash out of the World Cup against Germany!

Spain captain Iker Casillas lifts the World Cup after his country's 1-0 win over Holland!

Managers Jose Mourinho and Louis van Gaal get ready for the Champions League final between Inter Milan and Bayern Munich!

ACCESS ALL AREAS!

MATCH!
The funniest rumours and stories of the year!

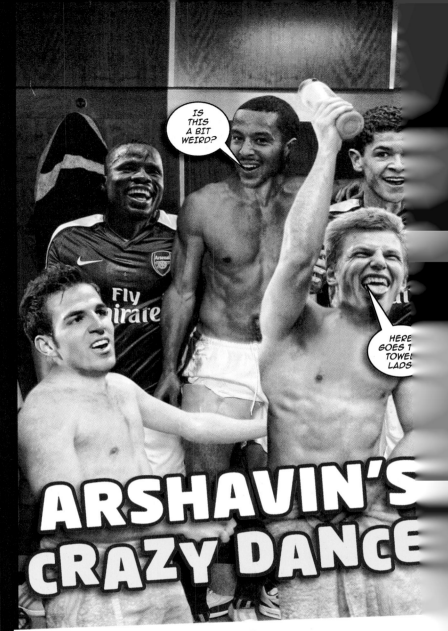

ARSHAVIN'S CRAZY DANCE

DIRK'S HAMMER TIME!

LIVERPOOL: Dirk Kuyt says he gets a doctor to smash him with a mallet twice a year to get rid of all the bumps he picks up on the footy pitch. The Reds star said, "You have to be a boss over your body!"

FERGIE'S NEW MATES!

MAN. UNITED: Check out Sir Alex Ferguson hanging out with some Canadian Indians. The guys from the Kwakwaka'wakw tribe visited United's training ground after they'd repaired an ancient totem pole in Manchester!

FRANCK'S PRANK!

YOU SHOULD SEE WHAT I DID TO ROBBEN!

THIS IS ONE FOR THE FAMILY ALBUM!

ARSENAL: Andrey Arshavin has revealed that Arsenal players dance around naked in the changing rooms after games. The lethal Russia forward says Emmanuel Eboue and Bacary Sagna always start the dancing, then all the other Gunners stars join in!

WE DO THIS EVERY WEEK!

BAYERN MUNICH: The Bundesliga giants had their official 2010-11 photoshoot in August, and legendary joker Franck Ribery made his young team-mate David Alaba look like a complete muppet!

CROUCHY kart king

I'VE GOT THE RED SHELL AGAIN! HAVE SOME OF THIS, DEFOE!

ENGLAND: Peter Crouch reckons he's a gaming legend at Mario Kart on the Nintendo DS. The England star plays eight-player link-up with his England team-mates!

FELLAINI'S BIG QUESTION!

IF YOU SIGN THIS I'M YOUR WIFE!

GET SOME SECURITY GUARDS IN HERE!

EVERTON: A mad Toffees fan asked Everton superstar Marouane Fellaini to marry her after an autograph signing session at Goodison Park, but the crazy-haired midfielder rejected the offer!

WORDFIT!

MY SCORE

50

Fit the names of these footy legends into this massive puzzle for tons of points!

FORLAN

Adam	Fabregas	Kuyt	Muller	Rooney
Bale	Given	Lampard	Nolan	Sneijder
Bent	Hangeland	Messi	Parker	Tevez
Dunne	Hart	Milner	Pienaar	Villa
Drogba	Ivanovic	Mourinho	Robben	Zamora

ANSWERS PAGE 94

MATCH!
THE No.1 FOOTBALL MAGAZINE!

ROONEY

FACTPACK!

Name:	Wayne Rooney
Club:	Man. United
Age:	24
Position:	Striker
Value:	£50 million

Did you know? Rooney won his first PFA Player Of The Year award in 2009-10!

CLASSIC MOMENTS OF 2010

Fulham	4-1	Juventus

Zamora 9
Gera 39, 49 (pen)
Dempsey 82

Trezeguet 2

Date: March 18
Stadium: Craven Cottage
Tournament: Europa League Last 16
What happened? David Trezeguet struck after just two minutes to put Juventus 4-1 ahead on aggregate, but Bobby Zamora and Zoltan Gera pulled Fulham level before Clint Dempsey's outrageous chip sealed the most famous victory in The Cottagers' history!

Fulham 4-1

Juventus

THE BIG QUIZ!

FLASHBACK!

Which Prem defender wants to forget this dodgy old pic?

THE STAR IS...

5 POINTS FOR CORRECT ANSWER

MY SCORE 5

MYSTERY FACTPACK!

Fill in the blanks in Yaya Toure's stat box!

Age:
Club: Man. City
Signed from:
Position: Midfielder
Boots: Nike T90 Laser III

5 POINTS FOR EACH CORRECT ANSWER

MY SCORE 10

5 QUESTIONS ON...

BAYERN MUNICH

1 How many Bundesliga titles have the German giants won – 20, 21 or 22?

2 What is Bayern Munich's nickname – The FBI, The CID, The FCB, The LOL or The FA?

3 Bayern Munich signed winger Arjen Robben from which massive European club?

4 At the start of which season did Bayern Munich move to their Allianz Arena stadium?

5 What's the name of the Dutch manager who took charge of the Bundesliga side in July 2009?

2 POINTS FOR EACH CORRECT ANSWER

MY SCORE 10

WHO'S THE BOSS?

Which top teams do these guys manage?

Nigel Clough

5 POINTS FOR EACH CORRECT ANSWER

MY SCORE 25

Neil Warnock

Roy Keane

Simon Grayson

Gordon Strachan

CROSSWORD!

Use the clues to fill in the giant crossword grid!

ACROSS

6. Jerome Boateng's country! (7)
7. Steve McClaren is the boss of this Bundesliga club! (9)
10. SPL club Robbie Keane joined on loan last season! (6)
14. Last season's beaten FA Cup finalists! (10)
15. England legend, ... Moore! (5)
17. Position of Man. United star Javier Hernandez! (7)
19. League 1 champs in 2010! (7)
20. Liverpool captain! (7)

DOWN

1. World Cup 2010 Golden Boot winner, Thomas ......! (6)
2. Serie A team who are nicknamed 'The Old Lady'! (8)
3. Fulham manager, Mark ......! (6)
4. Maicon's country! (6)
5. England beat this country 2-1 at Wembley in August! (7)
8. Scotland's first Euro 2012 qualifying opponents! (9)
9. Spain hero, Andres ....! (7)
11. Giant striker Peter Crouch plays for this Prem club! (9)
12. Former club of Stoke striker Kenwyne Jones! (10)
13. Liverpool's summer signing from Chelsea, Joe ....! (4)
16. The nickname of SPL club St. Mirren! (7)
18. Rangers' stadium! (5)

2 POINTS FOR EACH CORRECT ANSWER

MY SCORE 40

DEFENDER OR PRETENDER?

All of these players are top Prem stars, but which one doesn't play in defence?

THE PRETENDER IS...

10 POINTS FOR CORRECT ANSWER

MY SCORE 10

PHIL JAGIELKA
Everton

MICHAEL DAWSON
Tottenham

JOHN PANTSIL
Fulham

KIERAN GIBBS
Arsenal

YOSSI BENAYOUN
Chelsea

ANSWERS PAGE 94

Grab your popcorn and bucket of fizzy drink, because MATCH is heading to the cinema!

MOVIE MASH-UP!

POP CORN

FROM PRODUCERS TIM BURTON
AND TIMUR BEKMAMBETOV, THE DIRECTOR OF WANTED
AND VISIONARY DIRECTOR SHANE ACKER

9

WHEN OUR WORLD ENDED
THEIR MISSION BEGAN.
9-9-09

SCREENPLAY BY PAMELA PETTLER

FOCUS FEATURES

Fernando Torres

ASHL·E

06.27.08

Disney · PIXAR

Ashley Young

Joe Cole

Robinho

G.I. JOE
THE RISE OF COBRA
AUGUST 7
GIJOEMOVIE.COM

FROM
—LEY SCOTT
DIRECTOR OF
—ADIATOR

ROBINHO HOOD

FROM THE PRODUCER OF "PIRATES OF THE CARIBBEAN"

PRINCE OF PERSIE
THE SANDS OF TIME

Robin van Persie

MOVIE MADNESS

Man. United legend **Eric Cantona** quit footy in 1997 and became an actor! The crazy Frenchman has since had a part in Hollywood blockbuster **Elizabeth**, and starred in the film **Looking for Eric**!

MOVIE MASH-UP!

POP CORN

FA Cup

From the creators of NEMO & UP
THE BREAKOUT COMEDY OF THE SUMMER

Disney · PIXAR
ROY STORY 3

3D

2010

Disney · PIXAR

CUP

MAY 29
DISNEY DIGITAL
3D

Joe Hart

Roy Hodgson & Steven Gerrard

MOVIE MADNESS

Mexican actor **Kuno Becker** starred as Santiago Munez, a footballer who escapes the slums to become a star, in the film trilogy Goal. Footy legends **David Beckham** and **Zinedine Zidane** appear, too!

CRAZY HART

The most famous footy movie ever made was **Escape To Victory**. The World War II film starred Sylvester Stallone and Michael Caine and loads of footballers, including **Pele**, **Bobby Moore** and **Ossie Ardiles**.

Clint Dempsey

CLINT DEMPSEY IS

THE AMERICAN

FOCUS FEATURES PRESENTS THIS IS THAT/GREENLIT/SMOKEHOUSE PRODUCTION AN ANTON CORBIJN FILM GEORGE CLOONEY "THE AMERICAN" VIOLANTE PLACIDO THEKLA REUTEN PAOLO BONACELLI CASTING BEATRICE KRUGER COSTUME SUTTIRAT ANNE LARLARB MUSIC HERBERT GRÖNEMEYER EDITOR ANDREW HULME PRODUCTION MARK DIGBY PHOTOGRAPHY MARTIN RUHE EXECUTIVE ENZO SISTI PRODUCED ANNE CAREY JILL GREEN ANN WINGATE GRANT HESLOV GEORGE CLOONEY BASED ON THE NOVEL MARTIN BOOTH SCREENPLAY ROWAN JOFFE DIRECTED ANTON CORBIJN

THIS FILM IS NOT YET RATED. TheAmericanTheMovie.com FOCUS FEATURES

SEPTEMBER 1st

DISNEY'S A
CHRISTMAS CARROLL

IN THEATRES, DISNEY DIGITAL 3D, AND IMAX 3D.

Andy Carroll

CASINO REAL 7

NOVEMBER 17
www.CasinoRealeMovie.com

Xabi Alonso

WORDSEARCH!

Can you find the 20 world superstars hiding in the grid below?

```
Z U O S T Q H Z F H I M W F D U N W S H
D D L S E Y R K R N A M Q S X Z P A W I
R K J N P D W U J L F P E C K I G L R G
S A R D H L R R F Y X D F V L E V M V U
A Y I O F K Q O E K L H D I R G W I S A
Z I B W O I A N G A Y D L B B L M L W I
R T V V W S O K V B A P A D A P P I E N
D D T M U O Y V A A A F M R L H Z T V I
Y F E B R Q C A N Q M I E U O U O O E T
G R O N A L D O J Y M R S R T S Q N F O
C X T C Q C A S I L L A S I E E M R X R
N J Z S U T B L T W D G I C L X U C A R
S A D E B A Y O R W Q L B G L Z Y E V E
R O B B E N W T Q W A F V W I D Y K I S
F K D A S D F T A G O U R C U F F G F K
Z I P P L C R Q F O R L A N X B Y C P P
T D V Y V I L L A F I R B S X D C X M Y
G E R R A R D N D V K X G X W T H M M N
```

Adebayor	**Forlan**	**Kroos**	**Rooney**
Balotelli	**Gerrard**	**Messi**	**Torres**
Casillas	**Gourcuff**	**Milito**	**Valdes**
Drogba	**Higuain**	**Robben**	**Villa**
Fabregas	**Kaka**	**Ronaldo**	**Xavi**

ANSWERS PAGE 94

MATCH!
THE No.1 FOOTBALL MAGAZINE!

TEVEZ

FACTPACK!

Name: Carlos Tevez
Club: Man. City
Age: 26
Position: Striker
Value: £30 million
Did you know? He's worn the No.32 shirt at every Prem club he's played for!

THE TOP 10

WORST FACE FUZZ EVER!

I'M HAIRIER THAN AN APE!

10 TRIFON IVANOV
BULGARIA
Ivanov may have been in the Bulgaria side that finished fourth at World Cup 1994, but we can never forgive this dirty beard!

9 OLOF MELLBERG
OLYMPIAKOS & SWEDEN
The former Aston Villa and Juventus centre-back used to have a giant beard – it must have weighed more than a car!

I LOOK RUBBISH, DON'T I?

8 DAVID SEAMAN
ARSENAL & ENGLAND
The Gunners keeper won three titles and four FA Cups with this stupid tache stuck on his face!

7 DAVID BECKHAM
LA GALAXY
The ex-Man. United midfielder has always fancied himself as a fashion icon, but you could make a carpet with that gross beard. You've gotta sort it out, Becks!

THE GOATEE HIDES MY TRIPLE CHIN!

6 RAFA BENITEZ
INTER MILAN
In 2007, the former Liverpool boss grew this crazy goatee. Maybe that was the reason the Premier League club gave him the boot back in the summer?

YOU'RE THE BOSS!

MATCH is giving you a bank-busting **£1 billion** to spend on a world-class manager, a massive stadium and a team of stars! What kind of club can you build with your cash?

MANAGERS

SIR ALEX FERGUSON

Age: 68 **Country:** Scotland **Value:** £10 million

Fergie's been at Old Trafford since 1986 and still isn't ready to retire yet. He's won 46 trophies in his career, including 11 Prem titles, five FA Cups and two Champions League finals!

JOSE MOURINHO

Age: 47 **Country:** Portugal **Value:** £10 million

The Special One has won the league title in three different countries and became only the third manager in history to win the Champions League with two clubs last season!

PEP GUARDIOLA

Age: 39 **Country:** Spain **Value:** £8 million

Guardiola has built the best team in Europe since taking charge of Barcelona in 2008. He's won back-to-back La Liga titles and bagged the Champions League in his first season!

FABIO CAPELLO

Age: 64 **Country:** Italy **Value:** £6 million

England's gaffer had a stinker at the World Cup, but he's one of the best managers in footy history. Fabio won titles with AC Milan and Real Madrid before becoming Three Lions boss!

ROY HODGSON

Age: 64 **Country:** England **Value:** £1 million

Hodgson's our cheapest gaffer to pick from, but he's quality. The new Liverpool boss led Fulham to the Europa League final last season and has loads of managerial experience!

STADIUMS

OLD TRAFFORD

Club: Man. United **Capacity:** 76,000 **Value:** £200 million

Man. United's 'Theatre of Dreams' is the biggest club ground in England and even survived being bombed in the Second World War. Old Trafford also hosted the 2003 Champions League Final!

THE EMIRATES

Club: Arsenal **Capacity:** 60,355 **Value:** £400 million

Arsenal's stadium has one of the best pitches in the Premier League and the view from every seat is amazing. It cost The Gunners £390 million to build when it opened back in 2006!

SAN SIRO

Club: AC Milan & Inter Milan **Capacity:** 80,074 **Value:** £200 million

The most famous stadium in Serie A has hosted three Champions League finals and was also used at the 1990 World Cup. It's also known as 'Giuseppe Meazza', after a famous AC and Inter Milan star!

NOU CAMP

Club: Barcelona **Capacity:** 98,772 **Value:** £550 million

Barça's stadium is the largest in Europe and is always packed for home games. Man. United fans will never forget playing there in 1999, when they beat Bayern to win the treble!

ALLIANZ ARENA

Club: Bayern Munich & 1860 Munich **Capacity:** 69,901 **Value:** £350 million

The Allianz is one of the most amazing stadiums in the world. Depending on which Munich club is playing at home, the walls on the outside of the ground light up red or blue. It will also host the 2012 Champions League Final!

Allianz Arena

GOALKEEPERS

IKER CASILLAS

Club: Real Madrid **Age:** 29 **Country:** Spain **Value:** £25 million

Spain's captain had a great World Cup and conceded just two goals during the entire tournament. His one-on-one save against Holland's Arjen Robben in the final was vital!

PEPE REINA

Club: Liverpool **Age:** 28 **Country:** Spain **Value:** £15 million

Since moving to Anfield in 2005, Reina has become one of the Prem's greatest keepers. The Reds shot-stopper keeps tons of clean sheets every year, so Liverpool fans love him!

PETR CECH

Club: Chelsea **Age:** 28 **Country:** Czech Republic **Value:** £20 million

Chelsea's No.1 was in top form last season as Carlo Ancelotti's side stormed to a Prem and FA Cup double. Cech kept his 100th clean sheet in 2009-10 and saved a penalty in the FA Cup final!

EDWIN VAN DER SAR

Club: Man. United **Age:** 39 **Country:** Holland **Value:** £5 million

VDS didn't win any major trophies in 2009-10 and had an injury-hit season, but he's still a class act. He's the oldest Prem keeper, but his reflexes are still as sharp as ever!

JOE HART

Club: Man. City **Age:** 23 **Country:** England **Value:** £10 million

Hart took Shay Given's Man. City starting spot at the start of this season and has the talent to become the best keeper in the world. He could be England's No.1 for the next ten years!

CENTRAL

RICARDO CARVALHO

Club: Real Madrid **Age:** 32 **Country:** Portugal **Value:** £7 million

Injury problems and Alex's form kept the ex-Chelsea defender on the sidelines last season, so Carvalho teamed up with his old boss Jose Mourinho at Real Madrid in the summer!

NEMANJA VIDIC

Club: Man. United **Age:** 28 **Country:** Serbia **Value:** £30 million

Man. United fans were well happy when the Serbia star signed a new deal last season and ended talk of a move to Real Madrid. Vidic loves bossing strikers with his awesome strength!

THOMAS VERMAELEN

Club: Arsenal **Age:** 24 **Country:** Belgium **Value:** £10 million

The Verminator had an unforgettable first season with Arsenal. If he can strike up a decent partnership with new boy Laurent Koscielny, Arsenal could win their first trophy in five seasons!

JOHN TERRY

Club: Chelsea **Age:** 29 **Country:** England **Value:** £25 million

Despite problems off the field, JT still led Chelsea to the double in 2010. Terry's an inspirational captain and his power at the back makes him one of the Prem's most feared defenders!

CARLES PUYOL

Club: Barcelona **Age:** 32 **Country:** Spain **Value:** £12 million

Don't let Puyol's rubbish girly haircut fool you – the Nou Camp legend's one of the world's hardest defenders. His brave header in the World Cup semi-finals put Spain into their first ever final!

DEFENDERS

RIO FERDINAND

Club: Man. United **Age:** 31 **Country:** England **Value:** £18 million
Ferdinand's had no luck with injuries over the last few years and missed out on captaining England at the World Cup. But when Rio's fit, he owns strikers with his pace and tackling!

GERARD PIQUE

Club: Barcelona **Age:** 23 **Country:** Spain **Value:** £15 million
Spain's classy centre-back reads the game like a legend and was the key to Barcelona conceding just 24 goals in 2009-10. Pique also played every minute of Spain's World Cup win last summer!

LUCIO

Club: Inter Milan **Age:** 32 **Country:** Brazil **Value:** £10 million
A year after leaving Bayern Munich, Inter's centre-back helped the Serie A legends beat his former club to win the Champions League final. He kept 15 clean sheets as Inter won the treble!

GIORGIO CHIELLINI

Club: Juventus **Age:** 26 **Country:** Italy **Value:** £12 million
Juventus finished seventh in 2009-10 and Italy had a shocker at the World Cup, but Chiellini's still a big fans' favourite and was named Serie A's best defender for the second season in a row!

WALTER SAMUEL

Club: Inter Milan **Age:** 32 **Country:** Argentina **Value:** £10 million
Together with Lucio, the powerful Argentina centre-back had a season to remember in 2009-10 as Inter Milan charged to the treble thanks to his powerful headers and crunching tackles!

FULL-BACKS

MAICON

Club: Inter Milan **Age:** 29 **Country:** Brazil **Value:** £20 million
The powerful right-back popped up with some massive goals last season, including one in Inter's Champions League semi-final win over Barça, and Brazil's first against North Korea at the World Cup!

ASHLEY COLE

Club: Chelsea **Age:** 29 **Country:** England **Value:** £30 million
England's speedy left-back needs no introduction. Cole uses his pace to tear defenders to shreds, whips in deadly crosses and times tackles to perfection - he's one of the world's top defenders!

PHILIPP LAHM

Club: Bayern Munich **Age:** 26 **Country:** Germany **Value:** £18 million
With Germany captain Michael Ballack out injured, the Bayern star took over the armband to become his country's youngest ever World Cup skipper as they marched all the way to the semi-finals!

DANI ALVES

Club: Barcelona **Age:** 27 **Country:** Brazil **Value:** £25 million
We reckon Alves must forget he's a defender, because he spends so much time in the opposition's half. Attacking full-backs don't come any better than the Barcelona superstar - he's an assist king!

PATRICE EVRA

Club: Man. United **Age:** 29 **Country:** France **Value:** £20 million
Prem wingers must hate the sight of Evra, because the France star loves getting forward and played every league match in 2009-10. He even lifted the Carling Cup as Man. United captain in February!

FULL-BACKS

ERIC ABIDAL

Club: Barcelona **Age:** 31 **Country:** France **Value:** £10 million

Abidal faces a battle with Adriano for a starting spot this season, but he's still one of the best defenders around. He's won La Liga, the Ligue 1 title, the Copa del Rey and the Champions League!

BRANISLAV IVANOVIC

Club: Chelsea **Age:** 26 **Country:** Serbia **Value:** £15 million

With first-choice right-back Jose Bosingwa injured, Ivanovic made the spot his own and didn't look back. His devastating attacks from the back saw him named in the 2009-10 PFA Team Of The Season!

JAVIER ZANETTI

Club: Inter Milan **Age:** 37 **Country:** Argentina **Value:** £3 million

The Inter Milan legend set some massive records in 2010. Inter's awesome captain played his 500th Serie A match and lifted the Champions League trophy in his 700th appearance for the club!

SERGIO RAMOS

Club: Real Madrid **Age:** 24 **Country:** Spain **Value:** £25 million

The 24-year-old played at right-back and in the middle of Real's back four last season. Ramos also had more shots than any other defender in South Africa as Spain lifted the World Cup!

MATHIEU CHALME

Club: Bordeaux **Age:** 29 **Country:** France **Value:** £8 million

Bordeaux only finished sixth last season, but Chalme was in great form. The powerful right-back has played over 100 league games for the club and was linked with a move to Tottenham last season!

MIDFIELDERS

WESLEY SNEIJDER

Club: Inter Milan **Age:** 26 **Country:** Holland **Value:** £30 million
Was there a better midfielder in 2010 than the Holland and Inter star? Sneijder won the treble in his first season at the San Siro and reached the World Cup final, scoring five goals on the way!

STEVEN GERRARD

Club: Liverpool **Age:** 30 **Country:** England **Value:** £30 million
Liverpool didn't have a great season in 2009-10, but Gerrard's still an Anfield legend. Stevie G scored 12 goals and drove his team-mates forward with his awesome midfield engine!

FRANK LAMPARD

Club: Chelsea **Age:** 32 **Country:** England **Value:** £20 million
Lampard was in electric form last season, scoring 22 goals in 36 Prem matches as Chelsea won the double. No-one will ever forget his disallowed goal against Germany at the World Cup!

CESC FABREGAS

Club: Arsenal **Age:** 23 **Country:** Spain **Value:** £35 million
The Arsenal midfield star rips defences to shreds with his amazing passing! It was Fabregas who set up Spain team-mate Andres Iniesta for the winning goal in the World Cup final!

XAVI

Club: Barcelona **Age:** 30 **Country:** Spain **Value:** £40 million
There's no better playmaker on the planet than the Barça star. Xavi has amazing vision, his through-balls are unbelievable and he set up more goals than any other La Liga player in 2009-10!

MIDFIELDERS

ANDRES INIESTA

Club: Barcelona **Age:** 26 **Country:** Spain **Value:** £50 million
Despite having an injury-hit season in 2009-10, Iniesta still managed to play 20 matches as Barça retained the title. The highlight of his year was the winner in the World Cup final!

XABI ALONSO

Club: Real Madrid **Age:** 28 **Country:** Spain **Value:** £25 million
Liverpool fans must have wished Xabi was still at Anfield last season. His range of passing and rocket shots lit up La Liga as Real Madrid finished three points behind Barcelona!

BASTIAN SCHWEINSTEIGER

Club: Bayern Munich **Age:** 26 **Country:** Germany **Value:** £18 million
After moving from the wing to central midfield last season, Schweinsteiger masterminded Bayern's awesome displays, helping them to a League and Cup double and the Champions League final!

MARK VAN BOMMEL

Club: Bayern Munich **Age:** 33 **Country:** Holland **Value:** £6 million
Bayern Munich's rock-solid captain suffered a broken foot early last season, but stormed back to win the German double then reach the Champions League and World Cup finals!

ESTEBAN CAMBIASSO

Club: Inter Milan **Age:** 30 **Country:** Argentina **Value:** £10 million
Diego Maradona's decision not to name Cambiasso in Argentina's World Cup squad was one of the shocks of the year. He reads the game better than anyone and never gives the ball away in midfield!

WINGERS

CRISTIANO RONALDO

Club: Real Madrid **Age:** 25 **Country:** Portugal **Value:** £80 million

A lot was expected of Ronaldo after his world-record move from Man. United, and the winger delivered. Ronaldo scored 26 goals in 29 league games as Real Madrid finished second in La Liga!

FRANCK RIBERY

Club: Bayern Munich **Age:** 27 **Country:** France **Value:** £60 million

Ribery had a few moments to forget in 2010 as he was suspended for the Champions League final and got dumped out the World Cup in the group stage, but his silky dribbling can open up any defence!

ARJEN ROBBEN

Club: Bayern Munich **Age:** 26 **Country:** Holland **Value:** £35 million

Bayern's tricky winger turned defences inside out across Europe last season as they reached the Champions League final. Robben's volley against Man. United was one of the best goals of the year!

LIONEL MESSI

Club: Barcelona **Age:** 23 **Country:** Argentina **Value:** £120 million

Messi's still the world's greatest player! No defender can live with Leo when he runs with the ball and he scored an incredible 47 goals last season, including four in one game against Arsenal!

DAVID SILVA

Club: Man. City **Age:** 24 **Country:** Spain **Value:** £25 million

Full-backs are going to have nightmares about City's new wideman this season. The Spain winger loves whipping dangerous crosses into the box, so expect Mario Balotelli to score loads of headers!

WINGERS

ROBINHO
Club: AC Milan **Age:** 26 **Country:** Brazil **Value:** £20 million
Robinho struggled to settle in the Prem, but he's ready to rip it up in Serie A! The Samba skill king has more tricks than a magician and leaves defenders for dead when he turns on the style!

ANGEL DI MARIA
Club: Real Madrid **Age:** 22 **Country:** Argentina **Value:** £25 million
Mourinho's first signing as Real Madrid boss loves ripping up the left wing. Jose took a massive gamble on the 22-year-old who scored just ten goals last season, but he could become a Bernabeu legend!

MESUT OZIL
Club: Real Madrid **Age:** 21 **Country:** Germany **Value:** £20 million
Ozil shot to fame with a string of exciting displays for Germany at World Cup 2010, then joined Real Madrid from Werder Bremen in a bargain £12.4 million deal. Watch out for the playmaker in 2011!

FLORENT MALOUDA
Club: Chelsea **Age:** 30 **Country:** France **Value:** £18 million
Malouda had a tough start to life in the Prem after joining Chelsea from Lyon, but he's one of the top stars at Stamford Bridge now. He scored 12 goals in 26 Prem starts in their double-winning season!

ANTONIO VALENCIA
Club: Man. United **Age:** 25 **Country:** Ecuador **Value:** £18 million
Valencia's one of the best crossers of the ball in world footy and was named in the PFA Team Of The Season in 2009-10. He wants to get his hands on the Prem trophy for the first time this season!

STRIKERS

WAYNE ROONEY

Club: Man. United **Age:** 24 **Country:** England **Value:** £50 million

Rooney had a poor World Cup, but the Man. United striker buried 34 goals in all competitions last season, helping Red Devils fans forget all about Cristiano Ronaldo's £80 million move to Spain!

DIDIER DROGBA

Club: Chelsea **Age:** 32 **Country:** Ivory Coast **Value:** £20 million

Drog was in mind-blowing form in 2010 as he beat Wayne Rooney to win the Premier League Golden Boot with 29 goals. The Chelsea goal machine's strength, pace and heading are unbelievable!

FERNANDO TORRES

Club: Liverpool **Age:** 26 **Country:** Spain **Value:** £40 million

El Nino's had loads of injury problems, but he was Liverpool's top scorer with 18 goals in 20 Prem starts in 2009-10. Torres is fast, strong, skilful, deadly in the air and ice-cool in front of goal!

DIEGO FORLAN

Club: Atletico Madrid **Age:** 31 **Country:** Uruguay **Value:** £15 million

Forlan fired Uruguay into the World Cup semi-finals and bagged two goals against Fulham in the Europa League final. Loads of top clubs want to sign the Atletico striker, but they're desperate to keep him!

DIEGO MILITO

Club: Inter Milan **Age:** 31 **Country:** Argentina **Value:** £15 million

Milito proved he can destroy the world's best defences with loads of quality goals in 2009-10. He scored against Chelsea, Barça and Bayern Munich as Inter won the Champions League!

STRIKERS

DAVID VILLA

Club: Barcelona **Age:** 28 **Country:** Spain **Value:** £50 million
Villa's been one of the hottest strikers in Europe for nearly ten years. He's a natural goalscorer who always seems to score in the biggest games – he hit the net five times at the World Cup!

SAMUEL ETO'O

Club: Inter Milan **Age:** 29 **Country:** Cameroon **Value:** £25 million
Every player dreams of playing in the Champions League final, but Eto'o has starred in three. He netted 16 goals last season as Inter Milan lifted the trophy for the first time since 1965!

CARLOS TEVEZ

Club: Man. City **Age:** 26 **Country:** Argentina **Value:** £30 million
Tevez has been in red-hot form since moving across Manchester. He bagged 23 Prem goals last season and scored twice at the World Cup to stake his claim as one of the world's best strikers!

GONZALO HIGUAIN

Club: Real Madrid **Age:** 22 **Country:** Argentina **Value:** £25 million
Higuain's one of the best goal poachers on the planet. He scored 27 times last season, then became only the third Argentina player to bag a World Cup hat-trick with his treble against South Korea!

THOMAS MULLER

Club: Bayern Munich **Age:** 21 **Country:** Germany **Value:** £20 million
What a year Thomas Muller's had! Not only did he play in nearly every match for Bayern as they won the double, but he was only 20 years old when he picked up the Golden Boot at the World Cup!

DECISION TIME!

MANAGER: ....

STADIUM: ....

PICK A 4-4-2 FORMATION!

....

....

....

....

JUST FILL IN THE BOXES AND SEND YOUR TEAM TO THE ADDRESS BELOW!

TOTAL: £ ....

Send your selection to: **You're The Boss, MATCH Magazine, Media House, Lynchwood, Peterborough, PE2 6EA.** Send a photocopy if you don't want to wreck your MATCH Annual.

MATCH!
THE No.1 FOOTBALL MAGAZINE!

ROBBEN

FACTPACK!

Name: Arjen Robben
Club: Bayern Munich
Age: 26
Position: Winger
Value: £35 million
Did you know? Robben won the 2010 German Player Of The Year award!

Man. City	0-1	Tottenham
		Crouch 82

Date: May 5
Stadium: City Of Manchester
Tournament: Premier League
What happened? Tottenham travelled to Manchester knowing victory would book their place in the 2010-11 Champo League qualifying round, and they didn't let their fans down. Peter Crouch headed the only goal of the game eight minutes from time!

Man. City 0-

1 Tottenham

SPOT THE DIFFERENCE!

Find the ten changes we've made to these football pics!

ANSWERS PAGE 94

MATCH!
THE No.1 FOOTBALL MAGAZINE!

FACTPACK!

Name: Frank Lampard
Club: Chelsea
Age: 32
Position: Midfielder
Value: £20 million
Did you know? Lamps was the Prem's fifth top scorer in 2009-10 with 22 goals!

LAMPARD

they said wot?

MATCH remembers the best quotes and chants of the year!

"Pele should go back to the museum!"

Diego Maradona on Brazil legend Pele

"We've only got one Song!"

Arsenal fans sing about Alex Song

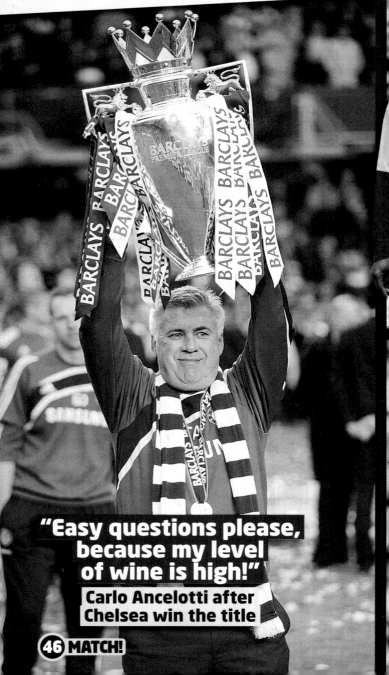

"Easy questions please, because my level of wine is high!"

Carlo Ancelotti after Chelsea win the title

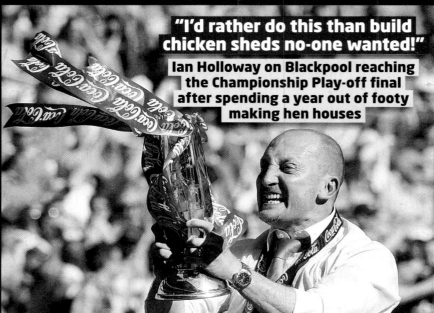

"I'd rather do this than build chicken sheds no-one wanted!"

Ian Holloway on Blackpool reaching the Championship Play-off final after spending a year out of footy making hen houses

"Thank you for helping me during the World Cup, but probably he is a little bit old!"
Fabio Capello ends David Beckham's England career

"He plays on the left, he plays centre mid, Charlie Adam could play for Madrid!"
Blackpool fans worship their midfield hero

"Sometimes you have a noisy neighbour. They will always be noisy. You just have to get on with your life, put your television on and turn it up a bit louder!"
Sir Alex Ferguson on Man. City

"I can guarantee we will finish in the top four!"
Ex-Liverpool boss Rafa Benitez's prediction doesn't quite come true

"Does your mummy know you're here?"
England supporters chant at Egypt fans back in March

"He is like a PlayStation player!"
Arsene Wenger on Lionel Messi after his four goals against Arsenal last season

FOOTY'S FUNNIEST

Top stars talk to MATCH about their fave footy memories!

CAN I HAVE A PAY RISE?

NAH, I'M THE KITMAN!

IS THIS LOOK NOT COOL?

MICAH RICHARDS
Man. City

MICAH SAYS: "When Sven-Goran Eriksson was our manager we played seven-a-side after training. At the end of the month our kitman did a presentation to the winners and dressed up like our old owner Thaksin Shinawatra. Everyone in the room was in stitches!"

WHERE DID YOU GET THAT JACKET?

I STOLE IT FROM A HOMELESS WOMAN!

JACK WILSHERE
Arsenal

JACK SAYS: "The funniest thing I've ever seen in football is the purple jacket Alex Song wore to an Arsenal fans' day. It was great!"

JERMAIN DEFOE
Tottenham

JERMAIN SAYS: "One of the Spurs physios was doing rehab with one of the players, so I got a ball and hit it. It was one of the best shots of my life, and as he turned around it smashed him right in the face. I killed him. As soon as it hit him he just collapsed on the floor!"

CHEERS, JD!

MOMENTS!

ANYONE WANT SOME FROZEN BOOTS?

GET YOUR SHORTS ON!

GRETAR STEINSSON
Bolton

GRETAR SAYS: "The best one was when my old team-mate at AZ Alkmaar Julian Jenner came into training wearing Ugg boots. We had to put them in the freezer, because I don't care what anyone tells you, they're women's shoes! They were totally ruined afterwards and he wasn't very happy!"

AARON LENNON
Tottenham

AARON SAYS: "There was a funny moment when Sebastien Bassong tried to get on the pitch without his shorts on. He had cycling shorts and a tracksuit on, but had left his shorts in the changing room. Harry Redknapp was furious!"

COME OVER HERE AND SAY THAT!

PLEASE DON'T KILL ME, DUNC!

ANYTIME, PAL!

JIMMY BULLARD
Hull

JIMMY SAYS: "The funniest moment that I was involved in was for Wigan against Everton. I was chatting to the Everton striker Duncan Ferguson just after he'd thrown Paul Scharner to the floor. He was a nutter, and I remember asking him a question and thinking, 'What's going on in his head?' It was a crazy moment!"

CLASSIC MOMENTS OF 2010

Blackpool	3-2	Cardiff
Adam 13		Chopra 9
Taylor-Fletcher 39		Ledley 36
Ormerod 45+1		

Date: May 22

Stadium: Wembley

Tournament: Championship Play-off Final

What happened? Ian Holloway's Blackpool side reached the Premier League for the first time in their history by coming from behind twice to beat Cardiff at Wembley. Brett Ormerod hit the winner in stoppage time at the end of an amazing first half!

WORDFIT!

Can you find the 20 Premier League players hiding in the massive puzzle below?

Adam	Fletcher	Lennon	Rodallega
Bendtner	Given	Milner	Skrtel
Carson	Heitinga	Nelsen	Taylor
Dann	Jones	Osman	Upson
Essien	Kranjcar	Piquionne	Van Damme

ANSWERS PAGE 94

MATCH!
THE No.1 FOOTBALL MAGAZINE!

unicef

FACTPACK!

Name: Lionel Messi
Club: Barcelona
Age: 23
Position: Forward
Value: £120 million
Did you know? Messi was named World and European Player Of The Year in 2009!

MESSI

TOP 10 TRANSFER SHOCKS!

10 ERIC CANTONA
LEEDS TO MAN. UNITED
Sir Alex Ferguson paid United's massive rivals £1.2 million for the France international back in 1992. No-one knew then that 'King Eric' would become an Old Trafford legend!

YOU'LL SIGN ME AGAIN IN 2010!

9 SOL CAMPBELL
TOTTENHAM TO ARSENAL
Campbell's getting on a bit now, but in 2001 he was one of the best defenders in Europe. Spurs fans hated the powerful centre-back for moving to their massive North London rivals!

8 MICHAEL OWEN
NEWCASTLE TO MAN. UNITED
The England striker had tons of injury problems at Newcastle and only scored 30 goals in four seasons, but Fergie still rated the striker and snapped him up on a free transfer last year!

I GOT ON THE WRONG TRAIN!

7 JONATHAN WOODGATE
NEWCASTLE TO REAL MADRID
The football world went into shock when Real signed Woody. The injury-hit centre-back took a year to make his debut in Spain, then scored an own goal and was sent off in his first La Liga game!

YOU CAN SEE MY AFRO FROM THE MOON!

6 DAVID JAMES
PORTSMOUTH TO BRISTOL CITY
Everyone thought the ancient keeper was moving to Celtic last summer, but he turned down a move to Parkhead to join the Championship club. Jamo then let in three goals on his City debut against newly-promoted Millwall!

I'LL BE THE AMERICAN PRESIDENT ONE DAY!

5 DAVID BECKHAM

REAL MADRID TO LA GALAXY

Becks turned down offers to return to the Prem in 2007 after falling out with Real Madrid boss Fabio Capello, then made a mad move to MLS club LA Galaxy!

4 JURGEN KLINSMANN

MONACO TO TOTTENHAM

Klinsmann was an incredible striker back in the early 1990s. After scoring five goals at the 1994 World Cup, Spurs shocked the Prem when they swooped for the Monaco hitman!

WE WON'T BE HERE LONG, CARLOS!

I'VE MADE A MASSIVE MISTAKE!

3 CARLOS TEVEZ & JAVIER MASCHERANO

CORINTHIANS TO WEST HAM

No-one could believe it when Tevez and Mascherano moved to Upton Park back in 2006. The Hammers were almost relegated that season, but Tevez's winner on the final day kept them up!

2 ROBINHO

REAL MADRID TO MAN. CITY

Everyone thought Robinho was heading to Chelsea in 2008, but late on transfer deadline day Man. City paid £32.5 million to sign the Brazil trickster and set a new British transfer record!

1 LUIS FIGO

BARCELONA TO REAL MADRID

Barça fans were furious when Figo joined their Spanish rivals Real Madrid for a world record £37.5 million fee back in 2000. The Portugal playmaker then went on to be crowned World Player Of The Year in 2001!

THE BEST AND WORST OF

WORLD CUP 2010

MATCH relives the greatest goals, craziest fans and most amazing stories from the biggest party on the planet!

GREAT GOALS!

GIO'S BELTER!
Gio van Bronckhorst slammed home a 35-yard screamer against Uruguay to put his side ahead in the World Cup semi-final!

TSHABALALA'S STUNNER!
What a way to score the World Cup's first goal! Soccer City erupted when Siphiwe Tshabalala ripped the top corner wide open!

FABIO'S CHIP!
Italy got dumped out in the group stage, but Fabio Quagliarella's cheeky chip from the edge of the area against Slovakia was world-class!

TEVEZ'S NET-BUSTER!
Carlos Tevez smashed a stunning 25-yard strike into the top corner as Argentina hammered Mexico 3-1 in the last 16!

SUAREZ TO THE RESCUE!
With the rain lashing down and the score level at 1-1, Uruguay hero Luis Suarez bent a shot into the net to see off South Korea!

COOL CELEBRATIONS!

SOUTH AFRICA
Tshabalala not only scored one of the best goals at the World Cup, the winger also joined his team-mates for a crazy touchline dance!

GHANA
The Black Stars lit up the World Cup on their way to the quarter-finals, and their dance celebration rocked!

BRAZIL
Brazil crushed Ivory Coast 3-0 in the Group Of Death, but do you remember Elano and Robinho's crazy jig?

CRAZY FANS!

HOLLAND

ARGENTINA

GHANA

ENGLAND

MASSIVE SHOCKS!

YAKUBU'S MISS!
Nigeria striker Yakubu missed the easiest chance of the World Cup when he fired wide from just three yards out!

UNBEATEN ALL WHITES!
Everyone thought New Zealand would lose every match, but Ricki Herbert's side played out of their skin and drew every group game!

ITALY GO HOME EARLY!
After two draws and a 3-2 defeat against Slovakia, World Cup holders Italy finished rock-bottom of Group F!

SWISS STUN SPAIN!
Midfielder Gelson Fernandes scored the only goal as Switzerland beat favourites Spain 1-0 in their opening game!

MADDEST MOMENTS!

PAUL THE OCTOPUS!
Eight-legged psychic Paul The Octopus became one of the stars of the World Cup by correctly predicting eight results!

JONG TAE SE'S TEARS!
It must be emotional to play at the World Cup, but that's no excuse for the North Korea striker to cry like a baby!

GREENO'S BIG MISTAKE!
Rob Green's World Cup dream ended when he let Clint Dempsey's shot slip through his hands against USA!

WORLD'S WORST TACKLE!
There was a lot at stake in the World Cup final, but we can't forgive this horror tackle by Nigel de Jong on Xabi Alonso!

DODGY DECISIONS!

FRANK LAMPARD v GERMANY

The England midfielder saw his chip hit the bar and drop two yards over the line, but the ref was the only one in the world who didn't see it!

LUIS SUAREZ v GHANA

Ghana looked to be heading into the semis, but Luis Suarez punched the ball off the line and Uruguay went through!

KAKA v IVORY COAST

Brazil's playmaker was sent off against Ivory Coast after Kader Keita pretended he'd been elbowed in the face!

CARLOS TEVEZ v MEXICO

Mexico's players went nuts when Carlos Tevez scored from an offside position and Argentina went on to win 3-1!

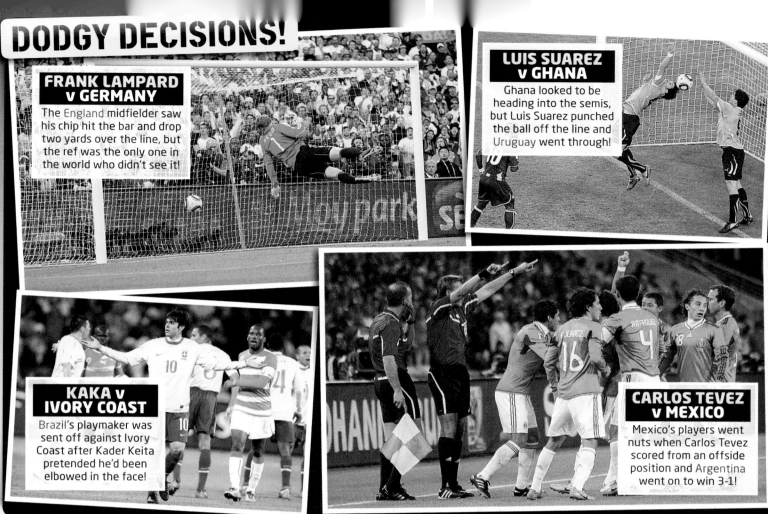

MEGA MATCHES!

SLOVAKIA 3
ITALY 2

This was the best game of the tournament! There were three goals in the final ten minutes as Italy crashed out!

GERMANY 4
ARGENTINA 0

Diego Maradona's stars had no answer to Germany's awesome attacking football in the quarter-finals!

GERMANY 4
ENGLAND 1

Joachim Low's side gave the Three Lions a football lesson as they tore England's dodgy back four to pieces!

HOLLAND 2
BRAZIL 1

Brazil took the lead with a great goal from Robinho, but Wesley Sneijder's double sent Holland into the semis!

DIEGO MARADONA!

We're going to miss Argentina's former boss, because he was a legend at the World Cup. With his attacking line-ups, crazy celebrations and weird training sessions, 2010 will always be remembered for Maradona!

Maradona makes a diving save in training!

Diego decides to show Javier Mascherano who's in charge!

Maradona takes cover as he gets pelted by flying footies!

It's all smiles as Argentina score against South Korea!

SURPRISE STARS!

KEISUKE HONDA

Arsene Wenger called the Japan playmaker a genius after watching his bullet free-kick and silky skills against Denmark!

DIEGO FORLAN

Four of the Uruguay striker's five goals in South Africa came from outside the area as he fired his country to the semis!

ASAMOAH GYAN

Ghana's powerful striker scored three goals in South Africa, including an unstoppable extra-time winner against USA!

BASTIAN SCHWEINSTEIGER

Schweinsteiger was the best holding midfielder at World Cup 2010 – he controlled games from the centre of the pitch!

GOAL MACHINES!

MIROSLAV KLOSE
The Germany legend proved he's one of the World Cup's greatest ever strikers with four awesome goals!

DAVID VILLA
The Barcelona star hit five goals, including three winners, as Spain stormed to their first world title!

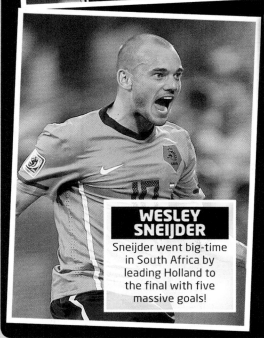

WESLEY SNEIJDER
Sneijder went big-time in South Africa by leading Holland to the final with five massive goals!

GONZALO HIGUAIN
The Argentina striker scored the only hat-trick of the tournament against South Korea!

THOMAS MULLER
Not many people knew the Bayern youngster before the World Cup, but he won the Golden Boot with five goals!

WORLD CUP FLOPS!

FRANCE
Out in the group stage, training ground bust-ups and Nicolas Anelka sent home - Les Bleus had their worst World Cup ever!

ITALY
Italy had loads of pressure on them as defending champions, and they folded under it by crashing out in the first round!

ENGLAND
Everyone thought England had a chance of winning the trophy, but they totally sucked as they were thrashed 4-1 by Germany!

SPAIN'S GLORY!

The European champions added the World Cup to their trophy cabinet for the first time after beating Holland 1-0 at Soccer City. Andres Iniesta's goal four minutes from the end of extra-time was enough to see captain Iker Casillas lift the famous trophy!

Iker Casillas kisses the trophy as Spain get ready to celebrate!

Liverpool star Fernando Torres gets his hands on the cup!

Ramos, Puyol, Fabregas, Pique and Busquets show off their medals!

Deadly striker David Villa poses for the camera!

Winger Jesus Navas looks like he's about to launch the World Cup at a photographer!

Andres Iniesta drills home the winning goal!

Andres Iniesta was named in FIFA's All-Star Team after an awesome tournament!

OH, AND THE VUVUZELA!

The Vuvuzela horn is one of the most annoying noises in the world, but it created a great atmosphere in South Africa. MATCH wants to hear it in the Premier League!

CROSSWORD!

Use all the footy clues below to complete this massive grid for 40 points!

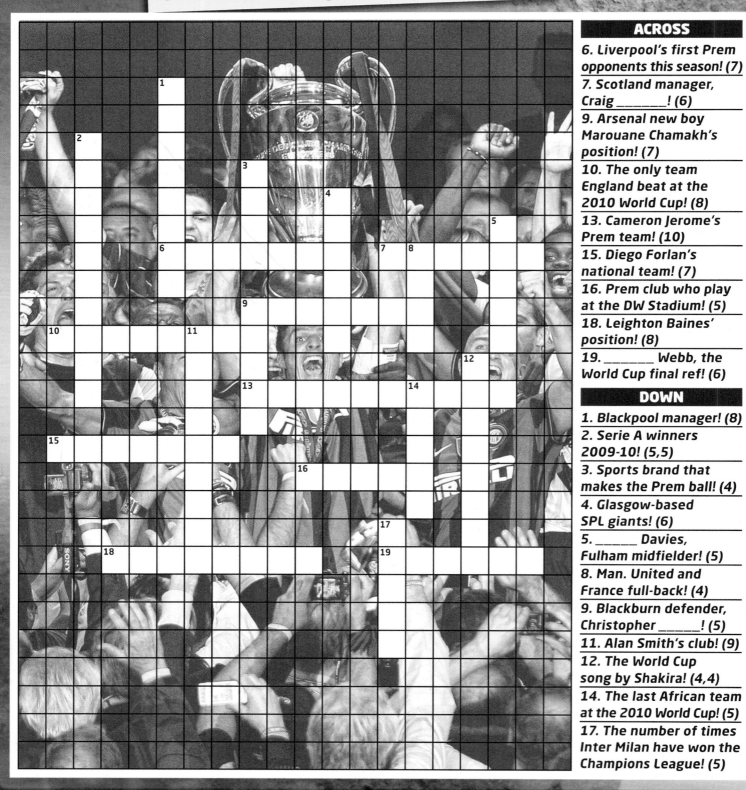

ACROSS

6. Liverpool's first Prem opponents this season! (7)
7. Scotland manager, Craig _____! (6)
9. Arsenal new boy Marouane Chamakh's position! (7)
10. The only team England beat at the 2010 World Cup! (8)
13. Cameron Jerome's Prem team! (10)
15. Diego Forlan's national team! (7)
16. Prem club who play at the DW Stadium! (5)
18. Leighton Baines' position! (8)
19. _____ Webb, the World Cup final ref! (6)

DOWN

1. Blackpool manager! (8)
2. Serie A winners 2009-10! (5,5)
3. Sports brand that makes the Prem ball! (4)
4. Glasgow-based SPL giants! (6)
5. _____ Davies, Fulham midfielder! (5)
8. Man. United and France full-back! (4)
9. Blackburn defender, Christopher _____! (5)
11. Alan Smith's club! (9)
12. The World Cup song by Shakira! (4,4)
14. The last African team at the 2010 World Cup! (5)
17. The number of times Inter Milan have won the Champions League! (5)

ANSWERS PAGE 94

MATCH!
THE No.1 FOOTBALL MAGAZINE!

RONALDO

FACTPACK!

Name: Cristiano Ronaldo
Club: Real Madrid
Age: 25
Position: Winger
Value: £80 million
Did you know? Ronaldo hit 26 goals in 28 league starts for Real in 2009-10!

CLASSIC MOMENTS OF 2010

Chelsea	1-0	Portsmouth

Drogba 59

Date: May 15

Stadium: Wembley

Tournament: FA Cup Final

What happened? Didier Drogba scored his seventh goal in a major cup final as Chelsea won the league and FA Cup double for the first time. Kevin-Prince Boateng and Frank Lampard both missed penalties in a crazy game that was settled by Drogba's free-kick!

Chelsea 1-0

Portsmouth

GAME LEGENDS!

Imagine a world where footballers were in console games!

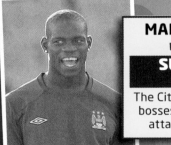

MARIO BALOTELLI
would be in...
SUPER MARIO GALAXY 2
The City striker loves battling bosses and using his deadly attacks to save the day!

DARREN BENT
would be in...
HALO: REACH
Sunderland's hitman is known for shooting on sight and always hitting the target!

GARETH BALE
would be in...
ASSASSIN'S CREED
The Wales and Tottenham winger loves sneaking up on opponents and surprising them with his lethal moves!

DIDIER DROGBA
would be in...
BIOSHOCK 2
Drog's strength and brutal attacks make him one of the Prem's toughest opponents, just like these Big Daddies!

JOE HART
would be in...
SPIDER-MAN: SHATTERED DIMENSIONS
The Man. City keeper's senses start tingling whenever he spots danger - he's always ready to swoop to the rescue!

CRISTIANO RONALDO
would be in...
TOY STORY 3
The Real Madrid superstar uses his lightning pace and sneaky tricks to get out of the tightest spots, just like Woody!

STEVEN GERRARD
would be in...
BATMAN: ARKHAM ASYLUM
Like Gotham City's crime fighter, Liverpool's skipper hates it when opponents cause trouble on his patch!

MAROUANE CHAMAKH
would be in...
POKÉPARK Wii
Arsenal's summer signing dresses in yellow like Pikachu, and uses his sizzling attacks to finish off opponents!

CARLOS TEVEZ
would be in...
LITTLE BIG PLANET

Just like tiny Sackboy, the Man. City striker has bags of energy and never stops running!

KEVIN NOLAN
would be in...
SIN AND PUNISHMENT

The Newcastle star knows how to lock-on to arch rivals and take down their attacks!

SIR ALEX FERGUSON
would be in...
LEGO HARRY POTTER

Harry and Fergie both wear specs, are tactical masterminds and can defeat any of their rivals!

CARLES PUYOL
would be in...
STREET FIGHTER IV

Blanka and Puyol have loads in common – they've both got crazy hair and love smashing opponents to pieces!

WORDSEARCH!

Can you find the 20 top world teams hiding in the massive grid below?

```
I P S I O M V Q U E S B R K N H B I L H
M N C V M S O E W A L A S A S R E A E Z
R L T C M A A N E C Z Y Z S Z R I A J R
F R I E H L N V Y M D E G H U O J K U T
Y Z U V R E D J R I J R D I M R I B K Y
P H U B E M L X W L F N W M X E N M Y V
L H R P I R I S T A C M L A L R G Y R R
Q X E O S N P L E N E U L A A B G M M X
R O A Z M V K O A A L N Z N G A U G A E
A S L C W O E A O N T I W T A R O S N F
N U M M U N A E Z L I C R L L C A I U P
G U A F N R M M U A C H P E A E N D N A
E M D J P N A H V E N S K R X L W D I J
R L R U E T H M H M I C R S Y O G S T A
S L I N D E P E N D I E N T E N K W E X
R Y D J H G J F K Z K A A O K A G C D M
C O L H S A O P A U L O R U O E A Q P C
H N H F O W W F L A M E N G O J Z G Q J
```

AC Milan	Celtic	Kashima Antlers	PSV
Ajax	Chelsea	LA Galaxy	Rangers
Barcelona	Flamengo	Liverpool	Real Madrid
Bayern Munich	Independiente	Lyon	Rubin Kazan
Beijing Guoan	Inter Milan	Man United	Sao Paulo

ANSWERS PAGE 94

MATCH!
THE No.1 FOOTBALL MAGAZINE!

FACTPACK!

Name: Steven Gerrard
Club: Liverpool
Age: 30
Position: Midfielder
Value: £30 million
Did you know? Gerrard made his 500th Liverpool appearance in 2009-10!

GERRARD

BEST OF 2010!

Patrice Evra regrets eating a pre-match curry!

Charles N'Zogbia looks well happy with Wigan's new signing!

YOU'RE PROBABLY BETTER IN GOAL THAN KIRKLAND!

HE CAN'T DO ANY WORSE THAN WE DID AT THE WORLD CUP!

When did Santa start playing for France?

YOU JUST TOOK A DUMP ON MY BACK DIDN'T YOU?

YEP!

Donald Duck wins his first cap for the Uruguay national team!

I DRINK TEN PINTS OF BACON GREASE BEFORE EVERY GAME!

Where did Liverpool star Joe Cole get that double chin from?

LET'S PARTY!

Joey Barton doesn't even get changed before a night out!

THE BIG QUIZ!

CLUB CAPTAINS!

Which teams do these stars skipper?

2 POINTS FOR EACH CORRECT ANSWER

MY SCORE 10

Carles Puyol

Kevin Davies

Massimo Ambrosini

Ian Evatt

Karl Henry

PREM REWIND!

Can you fill in the missing details from this season's clash between Aston Villa and West Ham?

ASTON VILLA...3
WEST HAM.......0
Aug. 14, 2010

5 POINTS FOR EACH CORRECT ANSWER

MY SCORE 10

15 MINS Downing
40 MINS
66 MINS

PLAYER MASH-UP!

5 POINTS FOR EACH CORRECT ANSWER

MY SCORE 15

Name the Prem stars in this weird pic?

Tottenham Hotspur

Birmingham City

5 QUESTIONS ON...

DIEGO FORLAN

1 What shirt number does Diego Forlan wear for Atletico Madrid – 7, 8 or 9?

2 How many times has the Uruguay striker won the European Golden Boot?

3 In what year did Diego sign for Premier League giants Man. United – 2002, 2004 or 2006?

4 Forlan has played for Atletico Madrid and which other massive Spanish club?

5 Diego won the Premier League, Community Shield and which other trophy while at Man. United?

3 POINTS FOR EACH CORRECT ANSWER

MY SCORE 15

WORDSEARCH!

We've hidden 20 team nicknames in this puzzle! Can you find them all?

```
C C C O I B X R U M M S J T O F E E S Z F C L B M K
F B Y R R J P L C S J S A I N T S I R X O F B H O Y S
C T T G Y X I X L B L M C R H S Y E B X G E J K Z Q T
F J H I C H E I S V L E F J N A T M H O R N E T S S J
O B V F J K V T Q S B B G O Y T Z D C W F I O B F F C
O Y R S M E A L D D Q O Q I J O V I L L A N S L Z O V A
M T A Y D C K R A T K L K P S C X D I A M S F C J F N
I Z G D K H I J G M P D R B H A M M E R S P Y R S K A
F A E C A B A J D R A I L W A Y M E N K F J G N I U R
E R A I E U X U O W B L K O K V J A M B O S E Y I S I
I L G U J X F Y X N D O P Z W A Z W T U D Z D S Y I E
B N L S X J D I V M M N J T S L N S Y I I A E C X L S
W B E G F D A G G E R S F J T Z S F U T X X I Y V K K
I U M B E A G L E S B U J L N E U J I K G M Q M U M F
L A Y V D W M G C G R N L D X C B C K A M C G S V E K
K S O K I N B J G O E W O F S W G B E S A E I U K N J
M P M D M A G P I E S D D Z P X H C V Y R G N V T H J
```

Bhoys	Citizens	Hornets	Owls	Saints	**2 POINTS FOR EACH CORRECT ANSWER**
Black Cats	Daggers	Jambos	Potters	Silkmen	**MY SCORE**
Bluebirds	Eagles	Lions	Railwaymen	Toffees	**40**
Canaries	Hammers	Magpies	Red Devils	Villans	

LA LIGA OR SERIE A?

2 POINTS FOR EACH CORRECT ANSWER

MY SCORE 10

Do these superstars play in Spain or Italy? There's ten easy points up for grabs!

Wesley Sneijder

Gonzalo Higuain

Luis Fabiano

Sulley Muntari

Andres Guardado

ANSWERS PAGE 94

SPOT THE DIFFERENCE!

Find the ten changes we've made to these football pics!

ANSWERS PAGE 94

MATCH!
THE No.1 FOOTBALL MAGAZINE!

FACTPACK!

Name: Wesley Sneijder
Club: Inter Milan
Age: 26
Position: Midfielder
Value: £30 million
Did you know? Sneijder has won the league title in Holland, Spain and Italy!

SNEIJDER

THE CRAZIEST MOMENTS OF 2010 YOU'D FORGOTTEN!

How many of the year's top stories can you remember?

LYON BEAT REAL!

After a 1-0 win in the first leg, Lyon silenced the Bernabeu as Miralem Pjanic's equaliser knocked Real Madrid out of the Champions League!

IT'S UNBELIEVABLE JEFF!

Soccer Saturday pundit Chris Kamara admitted he didn't see Portsmouth winger Anthony Vanden Borre get sent off against Blackburn!

SORRY, I WAS EATING MY DINNER!

IT'S ALL GONE WRONG!

CHELSEA CRUSH WIGAN!

The Blues needed a win to lift the Prem title, and they did it in style as they hammered Roberto Martinez's Wigan side 8-0 at Stamford Bridge!

THE DUTCH DESTROYER!

No-one gave FC Twente a chance under Steve McClaren, but the ex-England boss beat Ajax and PSV to the Eredivisie title in his second season!

DON'T MESS WITH JOSE!

OLD TRAFFORD IS FOR LOSERS!

TEVEZ SILENCES UNITED!

Carlos Tevez bagged a double against United in the Carling Cup semis, and the City fans loved it when he celebrated near the opposition dugout!

MOURINHO'S CELEBRATION!

Jose Mourinho couldn't hide his delight as Inter Milan beat Barça to reach the Champions League final. Barça were so mad they turned on the water sprinklers!

MANCINI AND MOYES GO MAD!

Man. City boss Roberto Mancini flipped out when he thought Everton's David Moyes was time-wasting at the end of their Prem clash in March!

I'M GONNA BURN THAT STUPID SCARF!

BENT SILENCES SPURS!

Darren Bent missed two penalties, but still scored two goals as he tore apart former club Tottenham's defence in a massive 3-1 win in April!

BECKS IS BACK!

AC Milan were crushed 4-0 by Man. United in the Champions League, but no-one will forget David Beckham's emotional return to Old Trafford!

PICK THAT ONE OUT!

ROSE'S ROCKET!

Danny Rose became a Spurs legend when he hit an unstoppable volley against Arsenal in the North London derby on his Prem debut!

SHOCK SIGNING!

Arsene Wenger did something he'd never done before – he re-signed a former player when defender Sol Campbell joined The Gunners in January!

WEST HAM UNITED

WHY ARE PEOPLE LAUGHING AT MY JACKET?

COZ IT LOOKS LIKE A DRESSING GOWN!

SULLIVAN   GOLD

THE WORLD'S WORST JACKET!

David Sullivan would look at home doing pantomime in the horrific pink blazer he wore after becoming one of West Ham's new owners!

BATTLE AT THE BRIDGE!

Man. City left-back Wayne Bridge refused to shake John Terry's hand after the Chelsea star was alleged to have had a fling with his ex-girlfriend!

1

2

3

MESSI'S ON FIRE!

The Barcelona magician scored four goals, including a hat-trick in an amazing 21-minute spell, to send Arsenal crashing out of the Champions League!

FA CUP SHOCKS!

Ex-Leeds striker Jermaine Beckford dumped massive rivals Man. United out of the FA Cup, while Liverpool lost to Championship side Reading!

JOSE'S RETURN!

Ex-Chelsea boss Jose Mourinho returned to Stamford Bridge with Inter Milan and finished The Blues' European dreams by masterminding a 1-0 victory!

WE'RE GOING TO WEMBLEY!

ROBBEN'S ROCKET!

Bayern Munich knocked Man. United out of the Champions League on away goals thanks to Arjen Robben's stunning volley at Old Trafford!

TEN-GOAL THRILLER!

Aston Villa reached their first major final since 2000 by beating Blackburn 6-4 at Villa Park in their Carling Cup semi-final second leg clash!

WHICH WAY TO THE BUFFET CAR?

CAPELLO LOSES IT!

Fabio flew into a rage at England's World Cup 2010 training camp after accusing snappers of taking pics of the team's medical room!

LIVERPOOL CATCH THE TRAIN!

With volcanic ash grounding most planes, Liverpool had to travel to Madrid by rail, road and air to play Atletico in the Europa League semi-finals!

YOU DON'T WANNA UPSET DON FABIO!

THIS IS TOO EASY!

BARCA TURN ON THE STYLE!

The match might have ended 2-2, but Barça's passing footy tore Arsenal to shreds in the first hour of their Champions League battle at the Emirates!

Inter Milan   **2-0**   **Bayern Munich**

Milito 35, 70

Date: May 22
Stadium: The Bernabeu
Tournament: Champions League Final
What happened? Argentina striker Diego Milito was Inter Milan's hero as they won the Champions League for the third time with a comfortable victory over Bayern Munich. It was Jose Mourinho's final game in charge of Inter before he left for Real Madrid!

2-0 Bayern

O REASONS WHY 2011 WILL ROCK!

Copa America!

There's no World Cup next year, but you can still get your international fix of Diego Forlan, Lionel Messi and Luis Fabiano in July when the 43rd Copa America kicks off in Argentina!

ENGLAND SCOTLAND

2012 Qualifiers!

The road to Poland and Ukraine is well underway and there are some mouth-watering matches next year. England head to Wales in March and Scotland face world champions Spain in October!

Transfer Time!

Last January saw Robbie Keane head to Celtic on loan and Adam Johnson move to Man. City for £7 million from Middlesbrough. What awesome big-money moves are going to happen this season?

Champions League Final!

Will Jose Mourinho become the first manager to win the Champions League with three different clubs, or will an English side wrestle it off The Special One? This year's final is at Wembley on May 28!

MATCH Magazine

Every Prem club is in MATCH every week and we'll have top interviews with Football League stars. Check out MATCH Results for stats and player ratings, too!

Under-21 Championship!

England face a battle to reach the finals in Denmark next June, but we'll be right behind Stuart Pearce's wonderkids, including Jack Wilshere, Micah Richards and Scott Loach!

Europa League!

Dublin's Aviva Stadium will host the 2011 Europa League Final. Fulham's run to the final in 2010 was class – will the tournament be as good this year?

Title Fight!

Chelsea won't give up the Prem trophy without a fight, but Man. United want it back and Man. City are desperate to prove they can scrap it out with the big boys!

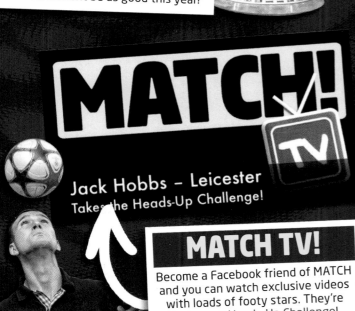

Jack Hobbs – Leicester
Takes the Heads-Up Challenge!

MATCH TV!

Become a Facebook friend of MATCH and you can watch exclusive videos with loads of footy stars. They're loving our Heads-Up Challenge!

MATCH Specials!

Keep checking MATCH for announcements of our special issues in 2011! They're packed with great gifts, posters, quizzes, cool gear and all the biggest stars!

QUIZ ANSWERS!

★ WORDFIT ★
PAGE 12

★ THE BIG QUIZ ★
PAGE 16

FLASHBACK!

Wes Brown.

MYSTERY FACTPACK!

Age: 27; From: Barcelona.

BAYERN QUIZ!

1. 22; 2. The FCB;
3. Real Madrid; 4. 2005;
5. Louis van Gaal.

WHO'S THE BOSS?

1. Clough – Derby; 2. Keane
– Ipswich; 3. Grayson –
Leeds; 4. Strachan – Boro;
5. Warnock – QPR.

CROSSWORD!

ACROSS: 6. Germany;
7. Wolfsburg; 10. Celtic;
14. Portsmouth; 15. Bobby;
17. Striker; 19. Norwich;
20. Gerrard. DOWN:
1. Muller; 2. Juventus;
3. Hughes; 4. Brazil;
5. Hungary; 8. Lithuania;
9. Iniesta; 11. Tottenham;
12. Sunderland; 13. Cole;
16. Buddies; 18. Ibrox.

DEFENDER OR PRETENDER?

Yossi Benayoun is
the pretender.

★ WORDSEARCH ★
PAGE 22

★ SPOT THE DIFFERENCE ★
PAGE 44

1. Victor Valdes' head has disappeared; 2. The white
logo on Valdes' sleeve has gone; 3. The hand using the
camera has gone; 4. Pedro's kit is now No.58; 5. David
Silva's medal ribbon is green; 6. Torres' gold medal has
gone; 7. Torres' tattoo has disappeared; 8. The head at
the back has disappeared; 9. The stripes are missing
from Iniesta's sleeve; 10. The Spain badge has gone.

★ WORDFIT ★
PAGE 52

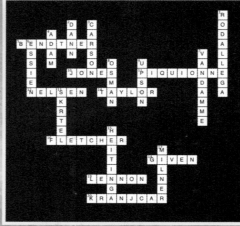

★ CROSSWORD ★
PAGE 64

★ WORDSEARCH ★
PAGE 72

★ THE BIG QUIZ ★
PAGE 78

CLUB CAPTAINS!

1. Puyol – Barcelona;
2. Davies – Bolton;
3. Ambrosini – AC Milan;
4. Evatt – Blackpool;
5. Henry – Wolves.

PLAYER MASH-UP!

1. Aaron Lennon; 2. Martin
Petrov; 3. Ben Foster.

PREM REWIND!

40 – Petrov; 66 – Milner.

DIEGO FORLAN QUIZ!

1. No.7; 2. Twice; 3. 2002;

4. Villarreal; 5. FA Cup.

WORDSEARCH!

LA LIGA OR SERIE A

1. Sneijder – Serie A;
2. Higuain – La Liga;
3. Fabiano – La Liga;
4. Muntari – Serie A;
5. Guardado – La Liga.

★ SPOT THE DIFFERENCE ★
PAGE 80

1. Fan's jacket is now yellow; 2. Anelka's boot has
disappeared; 3. Ball has turned yellow; 4. Portsmouth
player's head has disappeared; 5. Top of Lampard's
shorts are now white; 6. The badge on Malouda's shorts
has disappeared; 7. Malouda's collar is blue; 8. The
sponsor on Finnan's kit is now 'Jobhelp'; 9. Finnan's
shorts now say No.1; 10. One of the red fans has gone.

MY TOTAL: /450